New York Times
v.
United States
National Security and Censorship

New York Times v. United States

National Security and Censorship

D. J. Herda

Landmark Supreme Court Cases

ENSLOW PUBLISHERS, INC.

Bloy St. and Ramsey Ave.	P.O. Box 38
Box 777	Aldershot
Hillside, NJ 07205	Hants GU12 6BP
U.S.A.	U.K.

Library of Congress Cataloging-in-Publication Data

Herda, D.J., 1948-
    New York Times v. United States: national security and censorship / by D.J. Herda.
        p. cm. — (Landmark Supreme Court Cases)
    Includes bibliographical references and index.
    ISBN 0-89490-490-6
    1. New York Times (Firm) — Trials, litigation, etc. — Juvenile literature. 2. Pentagon
Papers — Juvenile literature. 3. Freedom of the press — United States — Juvenile
literature. 4. Security classification (Government documents) — United States —
Juvenile literature. I. Title. II. Series.
    KF228.N52H47 1994
    342.73'0853 — dc20   93-32156
    [347.302853]   CIP

Printed in the United States of America

10 9 8 7 6 5 4 3 2 1

Contents

1

The War in Vietnam

War was nothing new to the battle-torn Asian nation of Vietnam. It had been raging there for most of the country's history. Prior to World War II, before there even was a Vietnam, fighting there was widespread. The three countries that would eventually make up Vietnam—Tonkin and Annam in the north and Cochin-China in the south—had been warring over boundary disputes for decades.

Finally in 1945, a well-armed group of Indochinese, known as the Viet Minh led by a Soviet-trained communist named Ho Chi Minh, forced the Annamese emperor Bao Dai off the throne. The group promptly claimed all three countries as its own. Ho Chi Minh was made president of the new country, which was renamed the Republic of Vietnam.

But British forces in Cochin-China, reinforced by French troops in October 1945, soon drove the Viet Minh out of the south. The following June, France claimed Cochin-China as a republic of the French Union, naming Bao Dai as chief of state. Soon, fighting broke out between French and Viet Minh forces. Communist China, the Soviet Union, and other communist countries supported Ho Chi Minh's Viet Minh troops from the north. On the other side, Great Britain, the United States, and several other democratic countries supported Bao Dai's new government in the south. Meanwhile, Dai appointed Ngo Dinh Diem his new premier.

After nearly a decade of civil war, the fighting between the north and the south finally came to a halt on July 21, 1954. Following a long and complicated peace conference held in Geneva, Switzerland, an imaginary line was drawn across Vietnam. Ho Chi Minh would control the government in the north and Bao Dai would retain control of the government in the south. The conference also called for national elections to unite the two governments into one country. But when South Vietnam rejected North Vietnam's proposals to arrange for the elections, fighting once again broke out between the two nations.

By the end of his term of office in 1961, President Dwight D. Eisenhower was becoming increasingly concerned about the escalating war in Vietnam. He had recently received several classified military documents detailing the Soviet Union's military involvement in the country of Laos, which neighbors Vietnam. A small, well-armed group of North Vietnamese troops, called Viet Cong, slowly began invading South Vietnam. The group was using its bases in Laos to stage attacks against the government of South Vietnam. The Viet Cong's goal was to win the support of the people, overthrow the government of Diem, and unite South Vietnam with North Vietnam under communist rule. And it seemed as though the Viet Cong were winning. Unless the United States acted to stop the North Vietnamese, all of Southeastern Asia might soon fall to communism.

When John F. Kennedy won the presidential election in 1960, he met with outgoing President Eisenhower for a briefing on the war in Vietnam. At Eisenhower's suggestion, Kennedy agreed to send additional United States advisers and increase economic aid to South Vietnam to help the democratic government—now headed by Diem—defeat the North Vietnamese forces.

But despite increased United States aid, the Viet

Newly elected President John F. Kennedy is shown here stepping off of the official presidential airplane with First Lady Jacqueline Kennedy.

Cong continued their advances, slowly winning control of many of the small towns that dotted the South Vietnamese countryside. In order to stop the spread of communism, Kennedy had to stop the Viet Cong. In a speech to the American people early in 1961, Kennedy called Vietnam "a proving ground for democracy . . . " and a "test of American responsibility and determination."[1] Few Americans at the time had even heard of Vietnam, and fewer still cared about what was happening there.

Following his speech, the President called his closest advisers to a meeting to discuss the growing Vietnamese problem. Half of the advisors suggested that the United States continue sending Diem aid; the other half wanted the President to send United States combat troops to help in the fighting. Kennedy himself was not prepared to abandon Vietnam to communist forces. But neither was he ready to commit American troops to a war halfway around the world.[2] Besides, Congress would never authorize such an ambitious military venture, and he might not win support for the plan from the American people.

So in April 1961, Kennedy created a special task force to provide social, economic, political, and military aid to the South Vietnamese government. He agreed to support the strengthening of South Vietnam's army of one hundred and fifty thousand soldiers with an additional twenty thousand men. He also agreed to send an additional one hundred American military advisers to Vietnam, bringing the total number of Americans in that country to eight hundred.

The following month, Kennedy asked Vice President Lyndon B. Johnson to go on a fact-finding mission to Saigon, the capital of South Vietnam. There, after meeting with President Diem, Johnson learned just how serious the war was. Upon his return to America, the Vice President—who opposed the spread of communism as much as Kennedy did—announced that the loss of Vietnam to the communists would one day force America to fight "on the beaches of Waikiki [Hawaii]."

"The battle against communism," Johnson said, "must be joined in Southeast Asia with strength and determination . . . or the United States, inevitably, must surrender the Pacific and take up our defenses on our own shores."[3]

Meanwhile, Diem—a shrewd politician who was loved and admired in his native country—proposed to Kennedy that the United States support a plan to increase South Vietnam's military to two hundred thousand soldiers. That would mean more American advisers, more United States equipment, and more economic aid. In response, Kennedy sent one of his most highly regarded generals, Maxwell Taylor, to Saigon to study the situation more closely.

Upon his return, Taylor sent a classified message to Kennedy. In it he suggested that Kennedy send to Vietnam three squadrons of helicopters, manned by United States pilots, plus eight thousand soldiers acting as advisers. By having the soldiers pose as advisers, the United States could keep public knowledge of its military involvement in Vietnam to a minimum. That would be necessary partly to avoid a negative reaction from Congress and the American voters, and partly to comply with the provisions of the Geneva Accords. The Geneva Accords are international agreements that strictly prohibit military intervention in foreign countries.

Playing down the possibility that such action might lead to a long and drawn-out war between North Vietnam and the United States, Taylor went on to write, "North Vietnam is extremely vulnerable to conventional bombing. . . . There is no case for fearing a mass onslaught of communist manpower into South Vietnam and its neighboring states [Laos and Cambodia], particularly if our air power is allowed a free hand against logistical targets."[4]

Although still cautious about pouring massive quantities of United States aid and troops into Vietnam, Kennedy had to do something. Despite his outright

General Maxwell Taylor, one of President Kennedy's most well-regarded generals, was sent to Vietnam to study the situation there. His suggestions to the President upon his return helped Kennedy to keep public knowledge of our country's involvement in Vietnam to a minimum.

denials to the American public, the President approved the transfer to South Vietnam of several thousand more "advisers" backed by several hundred American pilots. The pilots were to begin flying secret combat missions out of Bienhoa, an air base just north of Saigon. The real purpose of the flights would be carefully disguised as training exercises for the South Vietnamese army.

Meanwhile a growing number of Washington-based agencies was keeping tabs on the developing Vietnamese war. They conducted detailed studies of the conflict as it unfolded, and they reached the conclusion that South Vietnam was winning. The communist regime, based in the North Vietnamese capital of Hanoi, could not possibly emerge victorious against the combined forces of South Vietnam and the United States. At least that's what the studies showed. But while all the studies and reports pointed to an eventual victory for South Vietnam, they failed to take into account one very important fact—the determination of the North Vietnamese communists to win.

The determination of the North Vietnamese showed itself in January 1963 at the battle of Ap Bac. There, South Vietnamese and United States troops attacked a small group of North Vietnamese soldiers and their supporters. Despite being outnumbered ten to one, the North Vietnamese not only held their ground, they turned back their attackers—killing several South Vietnamese soldiers and three American helicopter crew members in the process.

Ap Bac proved to be an embarrassment to Kennedy. So too did the American news media, which was beginning to pose indelicate questions such as: Why had the South Vietnamese lost to an undermanned army and what were American pilots doing in the battle? Kennedy, who was well skilled at sidestepping the questions of the press, could have imposed censorship on the media, thus preventing them from reporting all United States involvement in Vietnam. But that action would imply that there was a larger war going on than Kennedy was willing to admit.

Instead, Kennedy continued to deny American involvement. But in the meantime he poured more aid into Vietnam, assuming—as did his staff—that larger quantities of people, money, and material would produce greater results. Kennedy, of course, turned out to be wrong and even admitted so to one of his administrative assistants, Kenneth O'Donnell. O'Donnell said that Kennedy had told him that he planned to withdraw all American troops from Vietnam after his reelection in 1964.

But Kennedy was not to have that opportunity. He

would be killed by an assassin's bullet in 1963—less than one year before the upcoming Presidential election.

Following the assassination, Kennedy was succeeded to the presidency by Lyndon B. Johnson. Johnson, a Texas-born millionaire, was a large man whose wildly swinging moods matched his size. At times, according to author Stanley Karnow, Johnson could be "cruel and kind, violent and gentle, petty, generous, cunning, naive, crude, candid, and frankly dishonest."[5]

One thing that Johnson was not, was soft on communism. America, he firmly believed, was the beacon of liberty—a philosophy Johnson had inherited from the daring battle of the Alamo. At the Alamo a ragtag band of Texans fought to their deaths in an effort to gain independence from Mexico.

On November 24, 1963, just two days after Kennedy's assassination, Johnson instructed his aide Henry Cabot Lodge to "tell those generals in Saigon that Lyndon Johnson intends to stand by our word." Johnson then wrote a memo to the National Security Council, stating that the United States would help South Vietnam "win their contest against the externally directed and supported Communist conspiracy."[6]

Meanwhile in South Vietnam, President Diem had been killed just weeks before in a political coup, an uprising, against the government. Diem was replaced by a military council of South Vietnamese generals. The generals were eventually replaced by General Nguyen Khanh.

Anxious to learn more about the rapidly unraveling political situation in South Vietnam, Johnson sent Secretary of Defense Robert McNamara to Saigon. Upon his return, McNamara publicly boasted about how well South Vietnam was doing in its war against the north and Ho Chi Minh. But in a secret memo deliberately withheld from the press, the defense secretary reported to Johnson that the situation in South Vietnam was disturbing. He predicted that, unless the United States took immediate and strong action, South Vietnam could very well fall to the northern communists. He based his findings on the fact that the South Vietnamese army was losing more weapons to the North Vietnamese than it was capturing. The North Vietnamese also controlled more of the country's people and held more territory than Washington had previously believed.

Meanwhile the Joint Chiefs of Staff—the military leaders who control America's armed forces—issued a statement to Johnson declaring that South Vietnam was a key to America's world leadership. If the United States could not defeat communism in Asia, they warned, it would not be able to stop it in Africa and Latin America. In order to win, the leaders concluded, the United States had to expand the war into neighboring North Vietnam, Cambodia, and Laos. Johnson, though hesitant to expand the war and distrustful of most military men, reluctantly agreed.

By now Americans had come to realize that a real war was being waged in South Vietnam. American reporters were daily sending stories back to the United States, and television and radio crews combed Southeast Asia looking for dramatic accounts of brave American soldiers locked in deadly battle with the communists from North Vietnam.

By mid-1964 the total number of Americans living and working in South Vietnam topped one hundred thousand. The Americans taught the South Vietnamese how to breed pigs, dig fresh-water wells, and build better houses. They worked as doctors, school teachers, accountants, and mechanics. They even established an American radio station in Saigon. At the same time the Central Intelligence Agency (CIA) and a dozen other undercover agencies—including one whose duties included spying on other spies—were hard at work trying to uncover North Vietnam's plans to win the war.

Following his strong Presidential victory at the polls in November 1964, Johnson believed he finally had the support of the American people to expand United States involvement in the war in South Vietnam. By introducing massive American air and sea strikes against North Vietnam and bolstering the number of American ground troops already fighting in the south, he was convinced that he could bring the North Vietnamese government to its knees.

But Johnson learned the hard way, over the next four years, that an ever-increasing supply of arms and soldiers does not automatically result in military victory. By March 31, 1968, when Johnson announced that he would not seek a second full term as President, the North Vietnamese had still not been humbled. And the war that had now outlived the administrations of two American Presidents continued.

In 1968, Republican candidate Richard M. Nixon—like Johnson and Kennedy, a strong opponent to the spread of communism throughout Asia—ran for President on the promise that he had a secret plan to end the war in Vietnam. The United States, he insisted, would not only win, it would win with dignity and honor. Nixon's long political history, solid background as Vice-President under Eisenhower, and promise to end the war helped him to win a landslide victory in November. Now an anxious America waited for Nixon to make good on his promise.

Armed with recent information that forty thousand North Vietnamese troops were using bases in

Henry Kissinger, President Nixon's Assistant for National Security Affairs in 1969, met with the President, the Secretary of State, and the Secretary of Defense to plan a strategy to end the war in Vietnam.

neighboring Cambodia, Nixon decided to act. On March 16, 1969, he met with Presidential Assistant for National Security Affairs Henry Kissinger, Secretary of State William P. Rogers, and Secretary of Defense Melvin R. Laird. He told them that the "only way" to get the communists to negotiate an honorable end to the war was "to do something on the military front . . . something they will understand."[7] The very next day American planes began bombing Cambodia.

The bombings were a well-guarded secret from the start. The United States did not want to admit that it was attacking a foreign country whose neutrality it respected. The other countries involved in the military action played along with the United States. Cambodia's Prince Norodom Sihanouk, anxious to have the North Vietnamese removed from his land, said nothing of the raids for fear that they would end before the job was done. North Vietnam's Ho Chi Minh, not wanting to admit that the North Vietnamese had crossed the borders of their neighbor and were living and working in Cambodia, also did not complain.

But there was another reason for Nixon's secrecy—a growing antiwar sentiment in the United States. Nixon knew that if the bombings were made public, hundreds of thousands of Americans already tired of the war could rebel. Already antiwar protestors were marching on the

Capitol and throughout the streets of America. Nixon mistakenly believed that by keeping news of the bombings from the American public, he could win the war that much faster.[8]

But when a reporter for *The New York Times* learned about the Cambodian affair and wrote an article detailing the secret war being waged there, Americans began an uproar. Violent demonstrations erupted from coast to coast. Nixon was furious with *The Times* for releasing the story. The last thing he needed were more antiwar protests at home!

On May 14, in an effort to satisfy both Congress and the American people, Nixon delivered his first major television address on the subject of Vietnam. He told the nation that he had developed a proposal for a negotiated settlement to end the fighting and bring American troops home. He appealed for patience, saying that "the time has come for new initiatives."[9] Shortly thereafter he announced a program for the gradual withdrawal of a small number of American troops from South Vietnam. The following September he announced a second troop withdrawal; and in a televised address on November 3, he told the nation about a cooperative United States-South Vietnam plan to bring *all* United States troops home and turn the fighting back over to the South Vietnamese.

Secretly, Nixon hoped that the announced

withdrawals would convince the North Vietnamese that the United States was serious about ending the war. He also hoped the announcement would encourage them to come to the peace table, where he was convinced an honorable solution to the conflict could be worked out. But his plan was not to be.

Following the President's announcement of troop withdrawals, Ho Chi Minh assembled his advisers to devise a plan that would sweep North Vietnam to victory. The North Vietnamese had long assumed that they could "outwait" the United States for an end to the war. Now they decided the time was right to return to the use of the small guerilla bands of fighters that had earlier proved so effective in invading South Vietnam. Ho Chi Minh addressed his nation over Radio Hanoi, warning his people that despite Nixon's announcement of troop withdrawals, the war in the south was gearing up. The North Vietnamese people, he said, had to "be prepared to fight many years more" until the American enemy "gives up his aggressive design."[10]

As the war in South Vietnam heated up, Nixon decided to attack additional communist strongholds in Cambodia, this time using land forces. On the evening of April 30, 1970, as he addressed the nation about his new Cambodian "incursion," (attack) a United States and South Vietnamese force of twenty thousand men supported by American aircraft launched an attack against two major North Vietnamese bases in Cambodia.

The plan was a disaster from the start. Instead of finding tens of thousands of communist soldiers in the camps, the drive netted little more than United States frustration. Most of the North Vietnamese, having learned in advance of the coming attack, had fled Cambodia weeks earlier and were hard at work shifting their center of operations to the northernmost provinces of South Vietnam. The communists who remained were forced deeper into Cambodia, ultimately destabilizing it. Despite his promise to the American people that the peace they were seeking was in sight, Nixon had merely succeeded in lengthening the war.

Meanwhile the antiwar movement at home continued to grow. The press lashed out at Nixon, whom reporters said had gone back on his pledge to end the war. Throughout the entire country, teachers, lawyers, businesspeople, and clergy joined forces with students to protest the continuing war. The demonstrations came to a head on May 4, 1970, when protesting students at Ohio's Kent State University were met by members of Ohio's National Guard. Several guard members fired into a "rock-throwing mob," killing four youths.

The slayings sparked protests across the country. More than four hundred colleges and universities shut down as students and professors alike staged strikes. Nearly a hundred thousand demonstrators marched on Washington, encircling the White House and demanding Nixon's impeachment.

After a year and a half in office, Nixon—who had campaigned for the Presidency on a pledge to "end the war and win the peace"—found himself more deeply involved than ever. And his problems had only begun.

2

New York, 1971

The New York Times, like most of the nation's newspapers, had been running articles about the progress of the war in Vietnam for more than a decade. At first the articles were short pieces buried in the back of the paper. But as time went on and United States involvement in the war grew, the fighting finally became page-one headlines.

By 1971, after several failed political promises to bring the American troops home from the war, the fighting was more intense than ever. Numerous rounds of peace talks between the United States and North Vietnam had proved useless. It seemed as though United States involvement in the war, which had originally been expected to last from six months to a year, would drag on forever. No one in the country seemed to know exactly how America had gotten so deeply entangled in a war so many thousands of miles away. Worse still, no one seemed to know how to get the country out of the war. Few Americans yet understood the behind-the-scenes role that their government had played in getting their nation into what was quickly becoming America's most unpopular war ever.

Then early in 1971, *The New York Times* received from an anonymous source a huge number of classified, (secret for reasons of national security), memos that had been commissioned by the United States Department of Defense. The Department of Defense is housed in the Pentagon building in Washington, D.C. The memos came to be known as the Pentagon Papers. The memos outlined for the first time America's involvement in the war in Vietnam. They revealed how Johnson had secretly paved the way to use combat forces in Asia. They detailed how the President had avoided consulting Congress before committing both ground and air forces to the war. They even went so far as to explain how the United States had secretly shifted government funds toward the war effort.

These memos were especially surprising to the editors of *The Times*, because the waging of war is a task guaranteed only to Congress. No one politician—not even the President—has the authority to decide on his or her own to wage war. That's a guarantee that the writers of the United States Constitution built into the country's laws in order to prevent a single tyrant—such as Germany's Adolph Hitler or Italy's Benito Mussolini—from gaining too much power and plunging the country into war. In bypassing Congress and sending American troops to Vietnam, three American Presidents—Kennedy, Johnson, and Nixon—might have broken the law.

In May 1971, a group of *The Times* editors decided that in the best interests of the United States the material in the Pentagon Papers had to be published. The American people and Congress had to be informed of the "secret war" that the United States government had been waging in Vietnam. So on June 13, *The Times* published the first of a planned series of articles detailing some of the more than seven thousand pages of the report. The following day the newspaper published a second installment. The articles detailed just how deceitful the United States government had been.

Then on the evening of June 14, 1971, United States Attorney General John N. Mitchell, at the request of President Richard M. Nixon, sent a telegram to *The New York Times* requesting that the newspaper stop further publication of the articles based upon the Pentagon

It was United States Attorney General John M. Mitchell who, on the evening of June 14, 1971, at the request of President Nixon, sent a telegram to *The New York Times*. In the telegram he requested that the newspaper stop publishing their articles on the Pentagon Papers.

memos. Mitchell made his request on the grounds that such disclosures would cause "irreparable injury to the defense interests of the United States."[1]

In the telegram from Mitchell to *The New York Times* president and publisher Arthur Ochs Sulzberger, the Attorney General said:

> I have been advised by the Secretary of Defense that the material published in *The New York Times* on June 13, 14, 1971, captioned "Key Texts from Pentagon's Vietnam Study" contains information relating to the national defense of the United States and bears a top secret classification.
>
> As such, publication of this information is directly prohibited by the provisions of the Espionage Law, Title 18, United States Code, Section 793.

Both Mitchell and Pentagon spokesman Jerry W. Friedheim cited sections of the Espionage and Censorship Chapter of the Federal criminal code. Section 793 of that code states that

> . . . whoever having unauthorized possession of, access to, or control over any document, writing, code book . . . or information relating to the national defense which . . . could be used to the injury of the United States or to the advantage of any foreign nation, willfully communicates, delivers, transmits . . . the same to any person not entitled to receive it, or willfully retains the same and fails to deliver it to the officer or employee of the United States entitled to receive it . . . shall be fined not more than $10,000 or imprisoned not more than ten years, or both.[2]

The Defense Department admitted that its attorneys did not know for sure if *The Times* was guilty of violating the security codes, or if the guilty party was the only person who had first provided the information to the paper. The confusion was caused in part because there was no precedent — no similar case in history to compare it to — in order to establish guilt or innocence by *The Times*. Nothing quite like this had ever happened before.

Following receipt of Mitchell's telegram, *The Times* editors called an emergency meeting to discuss the issue. Within hours they delivered a statement saying that the newspaper would "respectfully decline" the request of the attorney general. *The Times* personnel said that they based their decision upon the belief that informing the American people of the material contained in the papers was in the people's best interests.[3] The next day *The Times* published the third installment of its Pentagon Papers series.

Meanwhile several senators and congressmen had read *The Times* excerpts. Democratic Senator George S. McGovern of South Dakota, who had co-sponsored a congressional measure to withdraw all American forces from Vietnam by the end of 1971, said the documents told a story of "almost incredible deception" of Congress and the American people by the highest officials in government, including the President.[4] He went on to say that he could not see how any senator could ever again believe that it was safe to permit the executive branch (the President) to make foreign policy decisions without first consulting with Congress.

Hugh Scott of Pennsylvania, the Republican Senate leader, said that the release of the documents was "a bad thing. It's a federal crime." But he described the contents of the secret papers as "very instructive and somewhat shocking."[5]

Representative Paul N. McCloskey, Jr., a Democratic congressman from California, said the papers showed "the issue of truthfulness in government is a problem as serious as that of ending the war itself." He went on to complain of "deceptive," "misleading," and "incomplete" briefings given to him during his recent visit to Southeast Asia, often while Army officials who knew the statements to be untrue stood silent in his presence. "This deception is not a matter of protecting secret information from the enemy," McCloskey complained. "The intention is to conceal information from the people of the United States as if *we* were the enemy."[6]

In March 1971, a public poll reported that confidence in Nixon's handling of the war had dropped to 34 percent—the lowest approval rating in Nixon's Presidency. A second survey showed that 51 percent of all

President Richard M. Nixon, shown here with Chief Justice Warren Burger, was openly criticized by members of the House of Representatives and the Senate for his war policies.

Americans believed the conflict was "morally wrong."[7] Members of the House and Senate were openly critical of Nixon and his war policies. On June 22, the Senate passed a nonbinding resolution calling for an end to the war and a complete withdrawal of all United States troops. Nixon ignored the call.

On June 15, 1971, the United States government filed a motion with the United States District Court for the Southern District of New York requesting a temporary restraining order and an injunction against *The New York Times*. The temporary restraining order was designed to stop immediately the publication of the articles while the court took the time it needed to consider issuing an injunction, a court order, to permanently prevent *The Times* from publishing the articles. That same day the court issued a temporary restraining order and a preliminary injunction, pending further review of the case.

It was a sweet—if temporary—victory for Nixon, who had had problems with the American press in the past and whose dislike of political reporters was well known. More importantly the groundwork for legal struggle had been laid. Now the next move was up to *The New York Times*.

3

A Case for the United States Government

Daniel Ellsberg was born on April 7, 1931, in Chicago, Illinois. He graduated *summa cum laude* from Harvard University and the University of Cambridge. He served in the United States Marine Corps and then, in 1959, joined the Rand Corporation—a research center located in Santa Monica, California.

In 1964 Ellsberg was one of a select group of brilliant young scholars—called "the whiz kids"—recruited by Robert McNamara to work for the Pentagon. Ellsberg joined the United States Department of Defense and the following year was sent to South Vietnam by the government. There he worked on a special team that had the mission of locating and identifying enemy spies. He did his job well.

But in time Ellsberg grew disillusioned by the progress of the war and returned to the States. In 1967 he rejoined the Rand Corporation while remaining an active consultant to the United States government on matters concerning the war in Vietnam. During this period he helped to develop a secret study of the making of American policies concerning the war—the so-called Pentagon Papers.

In 1970 Ellsberg left Rand to join in the antiwar movement protesting United States involvement in Vietnam. The more Ellsberg protested, the more he came to believe just how immoral the war in Vietnam was. He began asking himself what he could do to help stop the war. Then an idea dawned on him.

Ellsberg decided to leak the information in the Pentagon Papers to the press. Once the American people learned of Washington's undercover operations, they would be furious. They would demand an end to the war—immediately!

When *The New York Times* released the first installment of the Pentagon Papers—copies of the documents and memos Ellsberg had kept from his years spent working with the government—Nixon was furious. He immediately asked for an injunction demanding that

Daniel Ellsberg was one of a select group of brilliant young "whiz Kids" recruited to work for the Department of Defense, at the Pentagon building in Washington, D.C. His growing disillusionment with the war in Vietnam led him to "leak" government information about the war to the press.

The Times stop the publication of the documents. When the court refused, Nixon instructed his staff, "I want to know who is behind this and I want the most complete investigation that can be conducted. . . . I don't want excuses. I want results. I want it done, whatever the costs."[1]

Kissinger, who had consulted briefly with Ellsberg shortly before Nixon had taken office, told Nixon that he had always considered Ellsberg a "fanatic" and a "drug abuser."[2] Attorney General John Mitchell said that Ellsberg was part of a communist "conspiracy"[3] and suggested that he be tried for treason.

Nixon hastily called together a small group of loyal White House staff members, led by Presidential assistant Egil "Bud" Krogh and lawyer David Young, to investigate Ellsberg's leak of classified documents to the press. The undercover investigative unit was soon dubbed the "plumbers" because of their task—to plug the "leaks" in the White House. Nixon's special counsel, Charles Colson, enlisted other undercover operators such as Howard Hunt, who had once been with the CIA, and G. Gordon Liddy, a former Federal Bureau of Investigation (FBI) agent.

Hunt and the other "plumbers" decided to break into the home of Lewis Fielding, Ellsberg's California-based psychiatrist. They hoped to find in Fielding's files enough information on Ellsberg to discredit him in the eyes of the public. The same group of "plumbers" later invaded the Democratic National Committee headquarters in the Watergate building in Washington, D.C.—an act that would eventually lead to Nixon's resignation.

The illegal activities of Ellsberg proved once and for all—to Nixon's satisfaction—that the leftists, liberals, communists, and other opponents of the Vietnam War were dangerous anti-Americans who could not be trusted, who had to be stopped. Krogh summarized the feelings of power at the White House best when he said, "Anyone who opposes us, we'll destroy. As a matter of fact, anyone who doesn't support us, we'll destroy."[4]

But by mid-1971 Nixon had failed to convince either the American public or the press of the danger that Ellsberg's activities had presented to the nation. Just the opposite, many Americans viewed Ellsberg as a national hero, someone who was willing to place his own integrity on the line in order to do whatever he could to unmask the years of deceit and secrecy in the government and to help bring a speedy end to the war.

Toward that end, Ellsberg enjoyed only limited success. His actions spurred Nixon and the United States government to sue *The New York Times* officials in an effort to force the newspaper to stop publishing the

Pentagon Papers. But the war would continue for another two years before finally coming to a grudging halt with the signing of a peace agreement in Paris on January 27, 1973.

In the meantime, *The New York Times* found itself on the brink of battle. But this fight was not unfolding in a rice paddy halfway around the world; it was taking place in the courts. On June 15, 1971, the case of the *New York Times Company* v. *United States* began. The United States Justice Department, acting as the plaintiff—or the complaining party in the case—filed a motion seeking a temporary restraining order to prevent *The Times* from printing additional articles based upon the contents of the Pentagon Papers.

The suit was filed in the United States District Court for the Southern District of New York, presided over by District Judge Murray I. Gurfein. The primary attorney for the government was J. Fred Buzhardt, general counsel for the Department of Defense. Many others also worked on the case, including the Attorney General himself, John N. Mitchell; the Assistant Attorney General, Robert C. Mardian; and the United States Attorney for the Southern District of New York, Whitney North Seymour, Jr.

The Times, in turn, enlisted the aid of Alexander Bickel, a professor at the Yale School of Law. Bickel was well known in the courts of New York as a scholarly defender of the United States Constitution. *The Times* also hired Floyd Abrams, a well-known practicing attorney from New York City, to represent the newspaper in its legal battle. Bickel argued against the government's request for a restraining order.

Meanwhile the government insisted that the publication of the Pentagon Papers would jeopardize national security. There were classified documents in *The Times's* possession that could damage the ability of the United States to conduct its operations in the war in Vietnam. Some of the material might even prove harmful to United States workers stationed in foreign countries around the world. The United States maintained a vast network of spies and counterspies to obtain much of the information that went into compiling the Pentagon Papers. Should the wrong people read the documents, they might be able to unmask the true identity of some of these undercover operatives, thus placing them in extreme danger.

So the United States government wrote in its opening statement to the court:

This action has been commenced to preliminarily and permanently enjoin defendants and their agents from further disseminating documents consisting of forty-seven volumes entitled "History of U.S. Decision-Making Process on Vietnam Policy" [the Pentagon Papers]. Plaintiffs further seek to gain the recovery of the aforementioned documents from defendants. This memorandum is submitted in support of plaintiff's application for an Order temporarily restraining the defendants from further disseminating the aforementioned documents and requiring the delivery of the documents to this court pending the determination of plaintiff's motion for a preliminary injunction.[5]

The government specifically asked the court to order the return of the documents because, as of this time, it still had no idea of exactly what papers *The New York Times* officials had in their possession. The government's complaint continued:

Defendants are in possession of a forty-seven volume study entitled "History of United States Decision-Making Process on Vietnam Policy." This study is currently classified as "Top Secret—Sensitive" pursuant to the provision of Executive Order 10501. As defined in the Executive Order, top secret information is "that information or material, the defense aspect of which is paramount, and the unauthorized disclosure of which could result in exceptionally grave damage to the nation. . . ."

On June 13, 14, and 15, 1971, defendants published documents contained in the study. By telegram dated June 14, 1971, defendants were advised by the Attorney General of the United States that further publication of the contents of the study will cause irreparable injury to the defense interests of the United States. In the telegram, defendants were requested to cease publication of the contents of the study and to return the study to the Department of Defense. Defendants have expressed the intention to continue to publish documents contained in the study until they are restrained from doing so by an Order of this Court.

Section 793(d) of Title 18 of the United States Code provides for criminal penalties against a person who, while lawfully in possession of information relating to the national defense which could be used to the injury of the United States, willfully communicates that information to persons not entitled to receive it or willfully fails to deliver it, on demand, to the officer of the United States entitled to receive it. The applicability of Section 793(d) has not been restricted to criminal actions.

Further publication of the contents of the study and defendants' continued refusal to return all of the papers to the Department of Defense will constitute a violation of Section 793(d). Moreover, such publication will result in irreparable injury to the interests of the United States, for which there is no adequate remedy at law. An injury is deemed irreparable when it cannot be adequately compensated in damages due to the nature of the injury itself or where there exists no pecuniary standard for the measurement of the damages. Irreparable injury also means "that species of damage, whether great or small, that ought not to be submitted to on the one hand or inflicted on the other."

In [this] case, defendants will suffer no injury if they cease to publish the contents of the study in their possession pending the determination of plaintiff's motion for a preliminary injunction. On the other hand, the national interest of the United States may be seriously damaged if the defendants continue to publish the contents of the study. Under circumstances in which no injury will result to defendants from the cessation of publication of the study in their possession and irreparable injury may result to the United States, the granting of a temporary restraining Order is appropriate. For the foregoing reasons, the plaintiff's application for a temporary restraining Order pending the determination of its motion for a preliminary injunction should be granted. Plaintiff's application for an Order temporarily restraining the further publication of the contents of the study in defendants' possession should be granted.[6]

After the request for a temporary restraining order was received by Judge Gurfein, he responded the same day by granting the government the temporary order, saying that any temporary harm done to *The Times* by the order "is far outweighed by the irreparable harm that could be done to the interests of the United States"[7] if the newspaper were allowed to continue publishing the secret reports while the courts further considered the matter. But the judge stopped short of ordering *The Times* to turn the Pentagon Papers over to the government. He stated:

> At this stage of the proceeding, I do not direct *The New York Times* or the other defendants to produce the documents pending the outcome of the litigation. I do not believe that *The New York Times* will willfully disregard the spirit of our restraining order. I am restraining *The New York Times* and the other defendants, however, from publishing or further disseminating or disclosing the documents . . . pending

the hearing of the Government's application for a preliminary injunction.

The questions raised by this action [the Government's suit] are serious and fundamental. They involve not only matters of procedure, but matters of substance and . . . of constitutional implication as well. . . . I believe that the matter is so important and so involved with the history of the relationship between the security of the Government and a free press that a more thorough briefing than the parties have had an opportunity to do is required. . . .[8]

In response to Gurfein's ruling, *The Times*—in a newspaper article published the next morning—agreed to comply. "*The Times* will comply with the restraining order issued by Judge Murray I. Gurfein. *The Times* will present its arguments against a permanent injunction at the hearing scheduled for Friday."[9]

The next day, Thursday, June 17, the government asked the court to order *The Times* to produce its copy of the Pentagon Papers for inspection and copying. Judge Gurfein declined, stating that he was not about to tolerate a governmental fishing expedition into the files of any newspaper. In response, *The Times* instead agreed to turn over for the government's inspection a list of descriptive headings for those memos in the newspaper's possession. That seemed to satisfy the government—for the time being, at least.

But the government was about to receive a surprise. On the morning of Friday, June 18, the *Washington Post*

46

began publishing parts of the Pentagon Papers in a new series of articles. Now the government had not one, but two newspapers with which to deal. That same morning the hearing concerning a permanent injunction against *The New York Times* officials began in New York.

The Times's attorney Bickel quickly suggested that the hearing be dismissed because the case was moot—or did not merit a hearing—because the court's decision would have no practical effect on the actual controversy. Bickel based his request on the fact that, since another newspaper—*The Post*—had already begun the publication of the Pentagon Papers, the same action by *The Times* was no longer of any consequence.

In support of his motion, Bickel had submitted to the court an affidavit—or sworn written statement—by James L. Greenfield, a *New York Times* editor. The affidavit stated that *The Washington Post's* news service had already begun distributing articles based upon the Pentagon Papers to its hundreds of newspaper subscribers throughout the country. Furthermore the Associated Press (AP), which by now had received its own copies of the articles based upon the Pentagon Papers, was busy distributing them to its 8,500 newspaper, television, and radio subscribers around the world. And this was only the tip of the iceberg!

Greenfield wrote in the affidavit:

It is evident that the very material which is the subject of the restraining order is receiving nationwide and worldwide dissemination from sources other than *The Times.* If the restraining order continue[s] in effect, *The Times* will suffer irreparable pecuniary [financial] and professional damage in that once the documents are published . . . they will lose their newsworthy value to *The Times* as an exclusive story and will cause *The Times* to lose all benefit from the large sums of money, time and energy expended by *The Times* in compiling this story. In fact, if the order continues in effect, *The Times* alone will be restrained from publishing its own carefully compiled story.[10]

The government's lawyers, United States Attorney Whitney North Seymour and Assistant United States Attorney Michael D. Hess, insisted that the case against *The Times* was still valid—despite the publication of the Pentagon Papers by *The Washington Post* and other newspapers.

Your Honor, I am informed that Mr. Robert Mardian, who is the Assistant Attorney General of the United States in charge of the National Security Division, is here in court and he has informed us that these articles in *The Washington Post* will be reviewed by the Justice Department and action will be taken [against *The Post*] if it appears to be necessary.[11]

And, true enough, while the hearing was unfolding in New York, the government, concerned about *The Washington Post's* publication of the Pentagon Papers, brought legal action against the newspaper before Judge

Gerhard A. Gesell in the District Court of the District of Columbia. Gesell subsequently denied the government's request for a temporary restraining order, and that evening, the government appealed Gesell's decision. The Court of Appeals for the D.C. Circuit overturned Gesell and granted the government's request for a temporary restraining order by a 2-to-1 vote.

Meanwhile, Hess continued to argue the main thrust of the government's case against *The New York Times*. He argued that by publishing the Pentagon Papers, *The Times* was violating the national security interests of the United States, and by doing so, was guilty of a violation of law and required to cease all such publishing. It was a matter of national interest, Hess argued—pure and simple—and it superseded any right of the press to publish. Executive Order 10501, dealing with matters of national security and the need for secrecy, spelled that out.

Next, Whitney North Seymour, who had received permission from the court to share the oral argument on behalf of the government, addressed the bench.

> May it please the Court, as we see it, the issue in this proceeding is a very simple one, and that is whether, when an unauthorized person comes into possession of documents which have been classified under lawful procedures, that person may unilaterally declassify those documents in his sole discretion.
> The position of the Government in the proceeding is equally simple. These are stolen documents. They are

49

classified. They compromise our current military and defense plans and intelligence operations and jeopardize our international relations.

Contrary to some of the suggestions in counsel's argument [in *The Times's* defense], and in the brief, that what this amounts to is a bald attempt at suppression and censorship, we have attempted to approach the matter with the highest regard for the constitutional rights of all concerned and in an orderly, lawful process. . . .

We are now at the point where we are presenting the matter on the merits, and I think it is important to recognize at the outset that our sole purpose here is to present the evidence to the Court so that the matter can be decided impartially and objectively on the facts and on the merits and in accordance with the law.[12]

Following Seymour's very eloquent opening statement, the government went on to introduce various witnesses in support of its contention that the Pentagon Papers were highly sensitive military reports that needed to be classified. Seymour also reviewed with the witnesses the process for declassifying documents—that is, taking secret documents and downgrading their classification until they are available for review by the general public.

Dennis James Doolin, a witness for the government, relayed the process by which a document is declassified:

When either a declassification takes place or a downgrading in the classification takes place, a notice is sent to the original addresses, say, if it is a cable, for example, that is later downgraded, they are notified and the classification is changed on the document.

Other documents are downgraded at the end of set

calendar periods, three years, for example. Certain documents are downgraded until they become unclassified. So there is an established procedure and there are officers, for example, in the Department of State, in the office of the Secretary of Defense, in each of the military departments, the services, as well as the Joint Chiefs of Staff, there are historians and people to assist researchers, scholars on matters of this type.[13]

Seymour went on to ask if there might not be numerous documents within the Pentagon Papers that were classified as top secret, and Doolin agreed that there were. Then he added that some of them were among the documents that *The Times* had not yet published but intended to do so, with the court's permission.

Next the government called as a witness Admiral Francis J. Blouin of the United Stated Navy. Blouin, asked to comment about a particular article among the secret papers that *The Times* planned to publish, replied, "Well, I can say in open session here that there is a summary in that report which describes what happens, but then it goes on and gets into very intimate details on the command organization of the United States, and I feel that to go any farther in describing that or the forces involved and how they are generated is very definitely damaging to the best interests of the United States."[14]

Finally, the government called William Butts Macomber, the Deputy Undersecretary of State for Administration in the Department of State, to the stand.

Seymour asked him if, in his opinion, the publication of portions of the Pentagon Papers had already jeopardized international relations. Macomber replied,

> A historic and present absolute essential to the conduct of diplomacy is the capacity for governments to be able to deal in confidence with each other and to have confidence that when they are dealing in confidence, that confidence will not be violated.
>
> If governments cannot deal that way . . . the communication which is the lifeblood of diplomacy is cut off and in fact diplomacy is crippled very severely.
>
> This not only damages the capacity for the United States to pursue its security interests . . . but it damages the prospects that all nations seek to develop an enduring and just peace in the world.
>
> If we cannot communicate privately with each other, the diplomatic process, which is the best hope we have to achieve this just and lasting peace, will be denied not only to this country but to others. . . . [15]

Seymour then asked Macomber if he thought that disclosing some of the material within the Pentagon Papers might have any impact on diplomatic relations or treaty discussions with foreign governments.

"Yes, sir," Macomber replied. "It would have an adverse impact."[16]

At that point the government rested its case. Seymour sat down, secure in the knowledge that he had done a reasonably good job in presenting the government's case.

And to outsiders viewing the hearing, he would have been right. But one thing was certain: *The New York*

Times would have to go to some lengths to refute the expert testimony the government had presented. The big question now was: Could *The Times* do it?

4

A Case for The New York Times

As soon as the attorneys for *The Times* had been notified on June 15 that the government might sue the newspaper to stop publication of the Pentagon Papers, they began mapping out their strategy. The basis for the newspaper's defense was one of the most basic and sacred concepts in American law. It was the First Amendment to the United States Constitution, which states:

> Congress shall make no law respecting an establishment or religion, or prohibiting the free exercise thereof; or abridging the freedom of speech or of the press; or the right of the people peaceably to assemble, and to petition the Government for a redress of grievances.

By asking the court to issue an injunction prohibiting *The Times's* publication of the Pentagon Papers, the government was in violation of one of the most basic principles of the First Amendment—freedom of the press.

The Times's attorneys also intended to argue the point that, just because the government claims that some material is top secret, it is not necessarily so. There had been many cases over the years in which material marked "classified" had actually been kept from the public, not because releasing it might jeopardize national security, but because doing so might embarrass the government or make it look bad in the eyes of other governments or the American voters.

So on June 18, 1971, when *The Times's* attorneys Floyd Abrams, William E. Hegarty, Alexander M. Bickel, and Lawrence J. McKay entered the United States District Court of New York, they were prepared to deal with the government's arguments concerning *The Times's* tampering with classified material.

When Judge Gurfein made a comment in his opening remarks about the possibility that *The Times's* publication of the Pentagon Papers might result in a foreign government breaking some secret military code, Bickel replied,

Your Honor, if it is true, it is true then dealing with historical documents going back even forty years, fifteen, ten. Every newspaper has to be concerned whether it is going to break a code then, your Honor. . . .

It is common knowledge that the security of codes is insured by their being changed with extreme rapidity in very short order . . . there is nothing in there [the Pentagon Papers] less than three years old. To think that a document like that could possibly compromise a code is within my understanding and within the understanding of everybody at *The Times*, within the kind of common knowledge that anybody can be expected to have and that must govern the work of a newspaper.[1]

In response to Judge Gurfein's comment that he wished *The Times* and the government had simply gotten together and discussed the matter prior to *The Times* having published the documents, Bickel said,

. . .There are two reasons for that, your Honor, which I hope will commend themselves to you.

One reason we see is that it is utterly inconsistent with the First Amendment on any matters except with the rare exception of wartime activities when it is clear to everyone that the citizen, as such, cannot have a judgment that is reliable, or in . . . national crises, as during the Cuban missile crisis, when it is again evident on its face of things that the judgment, the news judgment of a newspaper, may get into dangerous areas.

With those exceptions, we cannot submit what we are going to print in a newspaper . . . to government approval.[2]

Bickel, within a few short moments, had struck at the

very heart of the government's suit. The material contained in the Pentagon Papers did not relate to a national crisis, and it was *not* being published during time of war—not officially, at least. So how could it be considered sensitive? Even though the United States was deeply involved in the ongoing conflict in Vietnam, war between the United States and North Vietnam had never officially been declared.

Then just as quickly, Bickel moved into another area of defense—that of exactly what material the government has a right to classify.

> . . . I am not claiming, for example, if in time of war or national emergency a troopship leaves New York Harbor and *The New York Times* takes it into its head to publish the date of departure and the date of arrival and the probable course, thus leading to the destruction of that ship, that is protected by the First Amendment. . . . But, your Honor, as applied to this case, as applied to the materials that have been published, to the materials that it was made clear we still have . . . the application to censor us on the circumstances of this case, on the grounds that the Government is discomfited and anything that discomfits the Government because it may be put in an unfavorable light with a foreign government as a result of internal political discussion—any application of censorship to us on that ground, which is how we view the case, is a flagrant violation of the First Amendment, in our view.[3]

From this point, Bickel and Hegarty cross-examined the government's witnesses, concentrating on the areas they stressed earlier. Then Bickel made his concluding remarks, and within a matter of a few hours, the case had been argued. Judge Gurfein suggested that the attorneys contact him at 11 A.M. the following day to see if he had yet reached a verdict.

The following morning, the attorneys did call Judge Gurfein. Yes, he told them, he had reached a decision. So on Saturday, June 19, Gurfein denied the government's motion for an injunction against *The Times*. But, still concerned about the damage that might be done to the government if the Pentagon Papers were published while the continuing legal action worked its way through the courts, Gurfein added, "The temporary restraining order will continue, however, until such time during the day as the Government may seek a stay from a Judge of the Court of Appeals for the Second Circuit."[4]

So, while *The Times* won its first-round bid to prevent the government from receiving an injunction, it lost its attempt to have the temporary restraining order lifted. In effect, *The Times* had won, but it still could not publish any more of the series that it had broken to the American public.

Within minutes of Judge Gurfein's decision, the attorneys for the government appealed the case to Judge Irving R. Kaufman of the Second Circuit Court of Appeals. Judge Kaufman, after reading the government's argument, granted a stay—or a postponement—of the lower court's decision until June 21.

On Monday, June 21, a three-judge court met to hear the appeal by the government. The court decided to continue the stay until the following day, Tuesday, June 22, so that a full panel of Second Circuit Court judges could review the case.

On June 22, Whitney North Seymour and Michael D. Hess argued the government's case for an injunction in the Second Circuit Court in New York before an eight-judge panel headed by Chief Justice Henry J. Friendly. At the same time, the attorneys for *The Times*—the same attorneys who had represented the newspaper in the lower court—made a motion before the appeals court to overturn the temporary restraining order so that the newspaper could resume publishing its series while the case was being heard.

At 5 P.M. on June 23, the Court of Appeals for the Second Circuit Court met to consider the case, and in a 5-to-3 decision, voted to send the case back to Judge Gurfein for further hearing, in light of additional evidence that the government had supplied to the court. It also upheld the temporary restraining order against *The Times.*

So while the government had not yet won its case, it had at least accomplished one of its goals—preventing

The New York Times officials from publishing any additional Pentagon Papers articles while the matter continued before the courts.

The following day, June 24, the attorneys for *The Times* filed a petition for a writ of certiorari, a request that would take their case against the government to the highest court—the United States Supreme Court. They also requested permission to present an oral argument of the case before the Supreme Court and filed an Application for Vacatur of Stay, requesting that the Court overturn the temporary restraining order upheld by the appeals court.

In its application for certiorari, *The Times's* attorney William Hegarty attempted to convince the Supreme Court that the newspaper's publication of the Pentagon Papers should not be restrained, because by this time a number of other newspapers around the country had begun publishing articles based upon the documents. By being restrained from doing likewise, *The Times* was being unfairly singled out and would suffer both loss of prestige and income. Among the written remarks Hegarty sent to John Marshall Harlan, Associate Justice of the Supreme Court, were the following:

> The district court denied the preliminary injunction after a hearing. By affidavits and the testimony of witnesses at the hearing, the Government attempted to

Associate Justice John M. Harlan received written remarks from *The New York Times*'s attorney, William Hegarty, regarding *The Times*'s inability to continue printing its articles, due to the ban imposed on the newspaper.

demonstrate that the publication of the material in question [the Pentagon Papers] should be restrained because it would gravely prejudice [or harm] the defense interests of the United States or result in irreparable injury to the United States. The district court found that the Government failed to sustain its burden [of proof]. Specifically, the district court directed the Government to present any document from the "History," the disclosure of which in the Government's judgment would irreparably harm the United States. The Government's affidavits and testimony . . . discussed several of the documents. The district court found either that disclosure of those specific documents would not be harmful [to the Government] or that any harm resulting from disclosure would be insufficient to override First Amendment interests. . . .

As a result of the decision of the Court of Appeals for the Second Circuit, the petitioner [*The Times*] continues to be enjoined [prevented] from publishing the historical documents and articles it seeks to print, and this prior restraint [restraining order] will continue for additional significant periods of time. A number of newspapers and news wire services have already published news stories which petitioner has been enjoined from printing. It is reasonable to expect that other publications will follow. The documents themselves have rapidly become increasingly public and unless immediate relief is granted and the petitioner is permitted to freely publish—as the District Court ordered—it will suffer irremediable harm. News no longer current is stale and of severely diminished intrinsic value.[5]

Toward the end of the eleven-page document, Hegarty went on to request that the Court promptly consider hearing oral arguments in the case, since the very timeliness of the materials *The Times* was seeking to publish and the seriousness of the matter at stake—freedom of the press—were crucial to the best interests of the citizens of the United States.

Following Hegarty's application for certiorari to the Supreme Court, the government responded with a request for certiorari of its own—this one against *The Washington Post*—along with a written memo opposing *The Times's* request that the Court overturn the temporary restraining order.

On Friday, June 25, 1971, the United States Supreme Court issued an order granting a petition for certiorari to *The Times* and setting the oral arguments for the following morning. The Court went on to state,

> The restraint imposed upon *The New York Times* by the Court of Appeals for the Second Circuit is continued, pending argument and decision in this case.
>
> For purposes of argument, this case is consolidated with *United States* v. the *Washington Post*, petition for certiorari this day granted. . . .[6]

Four justices—Hugo Black, William Douglas, William Brennan, and Thurgood Marshall—voted to have the temporary restraining order against *The Times* lifted and the case returned to the lower courts, but they were overruled by the majority.

So, in the end, *The New York Times* won half its battle. It had succeeded in having the United States

Justice William Brennan, along with three other Justices, Black, Douglas, and Marshall, voted to have the temporary restraining order against *The New York Times* lifted. However, their votes were overruled by the majority.

Supreme Court agree to hear the case, even though the Court, by a split decision, voted to continue the restraining order.

Now all that was left for *The New York Times* was the hard part. Next on the newspaper's agenda: presenting its case to the highest court in the land.

5

To the Highest Court

Both parties in the case—the United States government and *The New York Times*—were anxious to take their arguments to the Supreme Court. *The Times* wanted to prove once and for all that the government had no right to suppress news or censor a publication except, perhaps, during time of war or national emergency. The United States government, on the other hand, intended to show the American people and the world that it had complete authority to classify documents as it chose and to prevent those documents from being made public.

But the government had another even more compelling reasons for wanting to take the case to the Supreme Court. In the case of the *United States* v. *Washington Post*—the nearly identical case unfolding at the same time as *The Times* case—the results had been anything but identical to that of *The Times's* case.

The initial courtroom appearances of both newspapers had ended similarly. Judge Gurfein had ruled in New York against the government. Judge Gessell had done likewise in Washington, D.C.

The government then took both cases to the appeals court. The court in New York ruled against *The Times*, sending the case back to the lower court, and continuing the restraining order. But the court in D.C. ruled for *The Post*, lifting the restraining order and allowing the *Post* to resume publication of the documents.

If the government didn't move quickly to argue its case against both *The Times* and *The Post*, it might be too late. With dozens—or perhaps even hundreds—of newspapers planning on beginning their own Pentagon Papers' series soon, the government needed to have the highest court in the land place an injunction against the release of the documents. Once that occurred, it would be relatively simple to get all the other papers to stop publishing the series.

Much to the government's delight, once the Supreme Court had agreed to hear oral arguments in the case, the Court imposed identical restrictions on *The Post* and *The Times*. Neither newspaper was allowed to publish Pentagon Papers material that the government had included in a list it had earlier furnished the Court. The list contained items that the government considered "dangerous." Although the Court order allowed the two newspapers to publish any Pentagon Papers material not on the government's list, both newspapers declined. Newspaper personnel said that "printing an article whose content was dictated by government officials would amount to submitting to censorship,"[1] and that, they felt, was contrary to their First Amendment rights.

Meanwhile, the Supreme Court acknowledged the importance of *The Times* case by scheduling a rare Saturday session to hear the arguments. So on Saturday morning, June 26, attorneys for the government, including Erwin N. Griswold, joined *The Times's* attorney Alexander M. Bickel and *The Post's* attorney William R. Glendon inside the main chambers of the United States Supreme Court building in Washington, D.C., to argue their cases.

Griswold stated:

> It is important, I think, to get this case in perspective. The case, of course, raises important and difficult problems about the Constitutional right of free speech and of the free press. We have heard much about that from the press in the last two weeks. But it also raises important questions of the equally fundamental and important right of the government to function. Great emphasis has been put on the First Amendment, and rightly so, but there is also involved here a fundamental

question of separation of powers in the sense of the power and authority which the Constitution allocates to the President as chief executive and as Commander-in-Chief of the Army and Navy.

Involved in that there is also the question of the integrity of the institution of the Presidency, whether that institution, one of the three great powers under the separation of powers, can function effectively. . . . [2]

Then Justice Stewart commented to the Solicitor General, "Your case depends upon the claim, as I understand it, that the disclosure of this information would result in an immediate grave threat to the security of the United States of America."

The Solicitor General replied, "Yes, Mr. Justice."

Stewart continued, "However it [the information] was acquired, and however it was classified."

"Yes, Mr. Justice," Griswold agreed, "but I think the fact that it was obviously acquired improperly is not irrelevant in the consideration of that question. I repeat, obviously acquired improperly."[3]

After some bantering back and forth about whether or not the government would consider declassifying parts of the Pentagon Papers in the event that it won its case, Justice Stewart returned to his earlier questioning.

"Mr. Solicitor General . . . this brings me back to my original question of a few moments ago as to what the real basic issue in this case is. As I understand it, you are

Justice Potter Stewart questioned the Solicitor General of the United States in order to better understand what the U.S. government felt was the main issue behind their case. Stewart determined that the United States government felt disclosure of the information in the Pentagon Papers would endanger national security.

not claiming that you are entitled to an injunction simply or solely because this is classified material."

"No," replied Griswold.

"Nor do I understand it that you are claiming that you are entitled to an injunction because it was stolen from you, that it is your property. You are claiming rather and basically that whether or not it is classified or however it is classified, and however it was acquired by these newspapers, the public disclosure of this material would pose a grave and immediate danger to the security of the United States of America, period."

"Yes, Mr. Justice."

"Now, isn't that correct?"

"Yes, Mr. Justice."[4]

Griswold then went on to present the argument that, in his opinion, the Supreme Court should uphold the Second Circuit Court of Appeal's verdict and return *The Times* case to the lower court for further hearings. Griswold summed up his argument by talking once again about the grave danger in which the United States had been placed by the publication of some of the Pentagon Papers.

Although the government had presented its case for nearly an hour, the majority of its rationale—the major points of its case—could be summed up briefly.

United States Government's Arguments

1) The United States government based its case on the fact that the publication of material contained in the Pentagon Papers, in the government's point of view, would pose a "grave and immediate danger" to United States interests and welfare.

2) The government, while conceding that the case raised important questions about the First Amendment of the United States Constitution, insisted that the overriding consideration of the case was the delicate nature of the material published and how it would affect the welfare of the United States and its ability to conduct future negotiations with foreign governments.

3) The government referred to the "integrity of the institution of the Presidency" as something that needed to be preserved.

4) The government said that the illegal acquisition of the Pentagon Papers by *The New York Times* was a point worth the Court's consideration.

Following the government's opening arguments, Bickel addressed the court on behalf of *The New York Times*. He pointed out that although *The Times* began publishing the Pentagon Papers on the morning of June 13, it did not hear from the government until the evening of June 15—a full thirty-six hours after the paper ran its first installment. Just how sensitive could the materials have been, Bickel commented, if it took the government a day-and-a-half to respond to them and another day to get a court-ordered restraining order against *The Times*.

Furthermore, Bickel argued, Judge Gurfein, in looking for specific documents of the gravest importance to the nation's welfare, failed to find any.

> The record will clearly show that the judge's sole purpose. . . and continuously expressed intent was to provoke from the Government witnesses something specific, to achieve from them the degree of guidance that he felt he needed in order to penetrate this enormous record.
>
> It is our judgment, and it was his, that he got very little, perhaps almost nothing. . . .
>
> . . . I think the Government gave Judge Gurfein all it had.[5]

Bickel went on to summarize *The Times's* defense "on principles, as we view them, of the separation of powers, which we believe deny the existence of inherent

Presidential authority on which an injunction can be based. . . ."[6]

Bickel continued, saying that he doubted the President's authority extended so far as to be able to impose prior restraint upon the free press except in times of war or national emergency.

> As Chief Justice Hughes formulated it [in the case of *Near* v. *Minnesota,*] it referred to—actually it said—we would all assume that a prior restraint might be possible to prevent actual obstruction of the recruiting service, and this is the Chief Justice's language, or the publication of sailing dates of transport [ships], or the number and location of troops. I suppose that . . . on the sailing dates of ships and the location of troops, there is a very specific statute. It is 18 U.S.C. 794, which has not been cited against us, which is inapplicable, which is why it has not been cited against us, because that is not what we report. That is not in our paper. . . .
>
> Whatever that case may be, it cannot be this case . . . there is no applicable statute under which we [*The New York Times*] are covered. . . . [7]

Justice Stewart then broke into the conversation and said to Bickel, "Your standard [for deciding which material is too sensitive to publish] is that it has to be an extremely grave event to the nation and it has to be directly proximately caused by the publication."

"That is correct," Bickel replied.[8]

After several more minutes of questions and answers between the Justices and the attorney, Bickel concluded his arguments. Then William R. Glendon, the attorney representing the interests of the *Washington Post*, addressed the bench.

Glendon, quite eloquently, told of how both the New York and Washington lower court cases had gone, how both Judge Gurfein in New York and Judge Gessell in Washington had failed to grant the government an injunction against either *The Times* or *The Post* because the government was not able to convince either court of the immediate and grave danger posed by the publication of the Pentagon Papers. That was because, Glendon insisted, there were no dangerous secrets contained in the Pentagon Papers.

Chief Justice Warren Burger then inquired, "Can anyone know in any certain sense the consequences of disclosure of sources of information—for example, the upsetting of negotiations . . . in Paris [the Vietnam War peace talks] or possible negotiations that we don't know anything about in the release of war prisoners and that sort of thing?"

Glendon replied,

> Your Honor, I think if we are going to place possibilities or conjecture against suspension or abridgement of the First Amendment, the answer is obvious. . . . All that we have [in this case] does not justify suspending the First Amendment. Yet that is what has happened here. . . . Judge Gurfein used the words up in New York, and I

am sure used them respectfully, but he said when there is a security breach, people get the jitters. I think maybe the Government has a case of the jitters here. But that, I submit, does not warrant the stopping of the press on this matter. . . . [9]

Glendon continued this line of argument for nearly fifteen minutes until Chief Justice Burger commented that some of the Pentagon documents, classified in 1965, might no longer be subject to classification.

"That is correct, Your Honor, and furthermore, some of these documents which were classified go back to 1945. The documents are that ancient. . . . "[10]

Then Glendon struck at a particularly relevant point in the case—the government's insistence that the newspapers had illegally obtained the documents that were now in their possession, and by doing so were guilty of committing a crime.

> . . . the Government and the press . . . are naturally in opposite corners—the press is trying to get as much news as it can and the Government, particularly where it may be embarrassing or where [the Government] may be overly concerned or may feel [the news] is embarrassing or may, in Judge Gurfein's words, have the jitters, [the Government] is trying to prevent that sometimes. On other occasions, the Government engages itself in leaks, because some official will feel that in the public interest it is well for the public to know, and that overrides any particular judgment of security or classification.[11]

In short, Glendon had brought before the Court a

Chief Justice Warren Burger, in response to the United States government's claim the material contained in the Pentagon Papers should be "classified" or kept hidden from the public, responded that some of the material might no longer be classified.

strategy that had been used by Washington politicians for years. Whenever a sensitive story needed to be told—such as the story of allowing homosexuals to serve in the military or raising taxes on America's middle-class families—a President would often "leak" the story to the press. If the American people were strongly against the issue, the President would deny that it had been his idea. If the people were in favor of it, the President would step forward to claim the glory.

For many years, Washington had used this "double-standard" game of cat-and-mouse with the press. Now suddenly, the government was claiming that, because the Pentagon Papers had not come from official government sources, they had been obtained illegally.

Glendon continued:

> The record, Your Honors, will find is [filled] with instances where leaks of confidential, secret, and top-secret material have been given to the press, or the press has found them out and published them, and of course nothing has happened. I think that is significant because this is the sort of thing we feel we are talking about. . . . [12]

So *The Times* and *The Post* concluded their oral arguments, which revolved around six main points.

The New York Times's Arguments

1) From the slowness of the government's reaction to the initial publication of the Pentagon Papers, it seemed logical that the documents were not all that sensitive or critical to national security.

2) The lower courts failed to find that the government had produced even a single sensitive document contained among the Pentagon Papers.

3) Under the principle of the First Amendment's separation of powers, the President could not legally impose restraint upon the press except in times of war or national emergency, and that was not the case with the Pentagon Papers.

4) Both lower courts had failed to grant the government an injunction preventing *The Times* and *The Post* from publishing the Pentagon Papers.

5) The government had no legal basis for preventing the press from publishing news just because the news was embarrassing or uncomfortable to the government.

6) History was filled with newspapers publishing material that had been "leaked" to them unofficially, and no paper had ever before been forced to withhold publication of that material.

Following the petitioner's arguments, Solicitor General Griswold was granted a period of time for rebuttal, or the opportunity to respond to his opponent's arguments. In his rebuttal he argued that, although there were few—and possibly no—cases of prior restraint against the press in the past, one was merited in this case. The sensitive nature of the material, he argued, made that clear.

When Justice Stewart commented that prior restraint of publication by a newspaper was unconstitutional, Griswold admitted, "It is a very serious matter. There is no doubt about it, and so is the security of the United States a very serious matter. . . . "[13]

By the time Griswold had concluded his rebuttal, the justices were satisfied that they had heard everything they needed to hear in order to reach an opinion. So the Court adjourned, after which the justices met in conference to discuss the case until 6 P.M.

Meanwhile, the Court's final meeting for the 1970-1971 term was scheduled for Monday, June 28. If the Court was going to issue an opinion during this term, it would have to act quickly. And so it did.

6

The Decision

When Monday arrived, an anxious nation awaited the Supreme Court's decision. When the decision failed to come—and failed to come on Tuesday as well—some people began to speculate as to what was happening. During its arguments, the government had asked the Supreme Court to return the case to the lower courts for further hearings and to adopt a standard that would halt any publication of the material if "it will affect lives, it will affect the termination of the [Vietnam] war, if it will affect the progress of recovering our prisoners of war."[1]

Could the Court, people began to wonder, be considering doing just that? Is that what was causing the delay? Finally, on Wednesday, June 30, the Supreme Court met in a hastily called special session. At 2:30 P.M.

in a hushed courtroom, Chief Justice Warren E. Burger read the Court's decision. In a 6-to-3 split vote, the Justices found as follows:

> We granted certiorari . . . in these cases in which the United States seeks to enjoin *The New York Times* and *The Washington Post* from publishing the contents of a classified study entitled "History of U.S. Decision-Making Process on Vietnam Policy."
>
> Any system of prior restraints of expression comes to this Court bearing a heavy presumption against its constitutional validity. . . . The Government "thus carries a heavy burden of showing justification for the enforcement of such a restraint." *Organization for a Better Austin* v. *Keefe*—United States.—(1971). The District Court for the Southern District of New York in *The New York Times* case and the District Court for the District of Columbia and the Court of Appeals for the District of Columbia Circuit in *The Washington Post* case held that the Government had not met that burden. We agree.[2]

So the Supreme Court, in a monumental 6-to-3 split decision, voted to reject the government's appeal for a permanent injunction against *The New York Times* and *The Washington Post* and lifted the restraining orders against the newspapers.

Among the dissenters was the Chief Justice who, along with Associate Justices Harry A. Blackmun and John M. Harlan, defended their decision based upon the belief that the President had the unrestrained authority to prevent confidential materials affecting foreign policy

Associate Justice Harry Blackmun was among the dissenters on the Supreme Court who disagreed with the Court's decision in favor of *The New York Times*. He believed that the President had the unrestrained authority to prevent confidential matters affecting foreign policy from being published.

from being published in the press. Furthermore they felt that the "frenzied train of events"[3] in the cases had not given the lower courts enough time to consider the case and they voted to retain the restraints against the newspapers while sending the case back to the lower courts for additional hearings.

The six Justices who voted in favor of the newspapers broke down into two groups of three. The first group of Justices—William O. Douglas, Hugo L. Black, and Thurgood Marshall—held the "absolutist" view. They believed that the press may not be suppressed under any circumstances—no matter what the threat to national security might be.

The second group—Potter Stewart, Byron R. White, and William J. Brennan, Jr.—held the more common view that the press could be prevented from publishing only in the event of war or time of national emergency. They agreed that no such threat existed with the publication of the Pentagon Papers.[4]

In a clear reference to what he saw as the government's shady handling of the war in Vietnam, Justice Black stated in his opinion that publications such as *The Times* and the *Post* were exactly what the First Amendment was designed to protect.

Byron White, one of the Justices voting in favor of the newspaper, held the view that the press could be prevented from publishing only in the event of war, or in times of national emergency.

Paramount to the responsibilities of a free press is the duty to prevent any part of the government from deceiving the people and sending them off to distant lands to die of foreign fevers and foreign shot and shell.

In my view, far from deserving condemnation for their courageous reporting, *The New York Times* and *The Washington Post* and the other newspapers should be commended for serving the purpose that the Founding Fathers saw so clearly. In revealing the workings of Government that led to the Vietnam war, the newspapers nobly did precisely that which the founders hoped and trusted they would do. . . . [5]

Justice Douglas, in agreeing with Justice Black, said that the First Amendment's purpose is to prevent "governmental suppression of embarrassing information" and that the cases "constitute a flouting of the principles of the First Amendment. . . ."[6]

Justice Brennan, commenting on the temporary restraining order issued against the newspapers, said that the orders should not have been imposed because the government had referred to security problems that might occur only in the most general of terms.

Justice Stewart, in the concluding remarks of his opinion, said simply, "I cannot say that disclosure of any of [the documents] will surely result in direct, immediate, and irreparable damage to our Nation or its people. That being so, there can under the First Amendment be but one judicial resolution of the issues before us. . . ." [7]

Justice Hugo Black, in voting in favor of *The New York Times,* said that the First Amendment was meant to prevent the government from holding back potentially embarrassing information from the public.

Justice White, in concurring with the Court majority, likewise spent considerable time talking about the government's failure to show that the Pentagon Papers contained material that might be seriously damaging to the nation, while Justice Marshall addressed the question of the separation of powers:

> The Constitution provides that Congress shall make laws, the President execute laws, and courts interpret laws. . . . It did not provide for government by injunction in which the courts and the Executive can "make law" without regard to the action of Congress. . . .
>
> . . . it is clear that Congress has specifically rejected passing legislation that would have clearly given the President the power he seeks here and made the current activity of the newspapers unlawful. When Congress specifically declines to make conduct unlawful, it is not for this Court to re-decide those issues—to overrule Congress. . . . [8]

Meanwhile, Arthur Ochs Sulzberger, the president and publisher of *The New York Times*, said at a news conference held in New York that he "never really doubted that this day would come and that we'd win." His reaction was "complete joy and delight."[9]

On the other hand, United States Solicitor General Griswold was quoted as saying, "Maybe the newspapers will show a little restraint in the future."[10]

But the truth was closer to how Alexander M. Bickel, the Yale law professor who had argued the case for *The*

Justice Thurgood Marshall, shown here to the right of President Lyndon Baines Johnson, voted in favor of *The New York Times*. He stressed the fact that the United States Constitution provided for a separation of powers. This separation would prevent the President from gaining too much power, as in the case of withholding information from the nation.

Times, saw it. Bickel said in a telephone conversation with *The Times* that the ruling placed the press in a "stronger position"[11] and that in the future no Federal District Court Judge would issue a restraining order against a newspaper merely on the government's dissatisfaction with the paper's publication of a particular story.

So the first case ever in which a temporary restraining order was issued against a newspaper in the interest of "national security" had finally had its day in court. The outcome could not help but strengthen the First Amendment protections of freedom of the press.

7
Yesterday, Today, and Tomorrow

Censorship of the press has existed for much longer than has the United States. As early as 1515 A.D., the Roman Catholic Church at the Council of the Lateran decreed that no publication could be issued anywhere the Church had jurisdiction without first obtaining the written permission of the bishop or of the inquisitor of the diocese. Before long, the notion of censoring the press was widely accepted, and many civil governments throughout Europe adopted the policy. Some countries still censor their national press.

In England, the press fought long and hard over the years until, today, it enjoys nearly total liberty—at least during times of peace. During wartime, though, strict censorship is imposed over the British press.

America's Founding Fathers, hard at work drafting a new set of laws for an awakening nation, were well aware of the problems that the lack of a free press had caused in Europe. When the first ten amendments—called the Bill of Rights—were added to the original seven articles of the United States Constitution, freedom of the press was high on the list. The Constitution's framers knew from bitter experience that censorship of the press often led to government corruption. They realized that the best way to keep political corruption from happening in America was to keep the press free from governmental influence.

For more than two centuries, United States courts have jealously guarded the freedoms guaranteed within the First Amendment. The case for *The New York Times*, in the eyes of most working journalists, could not have ended differently. If the Court had decided against *The Times* and prevented it from publishing the Pentagon Papers—or even forced *The Times* to clear parts of the series with the government before publishing—the values of a free press would have been seriously jeopardized.

Freedom of the press does not mean that the government cannot withhold—or attempt to withhold—information from the press. Indeed, the government does so frequently, often on a daily basis. In

Arthur Ochs Sulzberger, the president and publisher of *The New York Times*, was victorious in his fight for freedom of the press. However, the battle between the press and the government will surely be a continuing concern for the future.

that regard, it has as much right to do so as any individual.

But freedom of the press does not mean, either, that the government can prevent the press from publishing news once the press has obtained the necessary information and means to do so.

Unfortunately, freedom of the press has not been high on every leader's list of democratic freedoms. During the late 1930s and early 1940s, the idea of a democratic republic, very much like the one we have here in the United States, preventing the press from freely publishing information on the workings of the government, was unheard of. Yet during those ten years in history, that is exactly what happened.

Led by a man who had been defeated for the office of president before finally filling that position in 1934, the government worked long and hard to conceal information from the press that would prove embarrassing or damaging to the government. In time the leader succeeded in turning the press into just one more arm of his administration. Soon the press was printing only the information that had first been cleared with the government, giving that government a free hand to run the country as it wished without the citizens learning of the corruption, vice, and hysteria that were slowly sweeping the government.

By the time this man's administration had been forced from power, millions of people had died. Hundreds of thousands more were left homeless. And one of the bloodiest eras in world history had come to a sad and bitter end.

These events occurred in Nazi Germany. The leader was Adolph Hitler. And the world, some half a century later, is still struggling to recover.

Some people say that such a tragedy could never happen in America. Others believe that one of the only things preventing this tragedy from happening in America is a free press.

Chapter Notes

Chapter 1

1. Stanley Karnow, *Vietnam: A History* (New York: Viking, 1991), p. 264.

2. Ibid., p. 267.

3. Ibid.

4. Ibid., p. 269.

5. Ibid., p. 335.

6. Ibid., p. 339.

7. Ibid., p. 606.

8. Ibid., p. 607.

9. Funk and Wagnalls Standard Reference Encyclopedia Yearbook 1969 (New York: Funk and Wagnalls, 1969), p. 371.

10. Funk and Wagnalls Standard Reference Encyclopedia Yearbook 1970 (New York: Funk and Wagnalls, 1970), p. 533.

Chapter 2

1. *The New York Times* (June 14, 1971), p. 1.

2. Ibid.

3. Ibid.

4. Ibid., p. 18.

5. Ibid.

6. Ibid.

7. Stanley Karnow, *Vietnam: A History* (New York: Viking, 1991), p. 647.

Chapter 3

1. Stanley Karnow, *Vietnam: A History* (New York: Viking, 1991),p. 648.

2. Ibid.

3. Ibid.

4. Ibid., p. 649.

5. *United States of America* v. *New York Times Company*, et al. (Preliminary Statement, United States District Court, Southern District of New York, June 15, 1971), pp. 1-2.

6. *United States of America* v. *New York Times Company*, et al. (Argument, United States District Court, Southern District of New York, June 15, 1971), pp. 3-7.

7. "Judge, at Request of U.S., Halts Times Vietnam Series Four Days Pending Hearing on Injunction" (*The New York Times*, June 16, 1971), p. 1-1.

8. *United States of America* v. *New York Times Company*, et al. (Memorandum from United States District Judge Murray I. Gurfein, June 15, 1971), pp. 2-3.

9. "Judge, at Request of U.S., Halts Times Vietnam Series Four Days Pending Hearing on Injunction" (The New York Times), p. 1-1.

10. *United States of America* v. *New York Times Company*, et al. (Affidavit of James L. Greenfield, United States District Court, Southern District of New York, 71 Civ. 2662, June 18, 1971), pp. 3-4.

11. *United States of America* v. *New York Times Company*, et al. (Oral Arguments, United States District Court, Southern District of New York, 71 Civ. 2662, June 19, 1971), p. 17.

12. Ibid., pp. 31-32.

13. Ibid., pp. 71-72.

14. Ibid., p. 103.

15. Ibid., p. 112.

16. Ibid., p. 113.

Chapter 4

1. *United States of America* v. *New York Times Company*, et al. (Oral Arguments, United States District Court, Southern District of New York, 71 Civ. 2662, June 19, 1971), pp. 22-24.

2. Ibid.

3. Ibid., pp. 28-29.

4. *United States of America* v. *New York Times Company*, et al. (Opinion, United States District Court, Southern District of New York, 71 Civ. 2662, June 19, 1971), p. 16.

5. *United States of America* v. *New York Times Company*, et al. (Application for Vacatur of Stay, U.S. Supreme Court, June 24, 1971), pp. 8-9.

6. *United States of America* v. *New York Times Company,* et al. (Order, U.S. Supreme Court, No. 1873, June 25, 1971).

Chapter 5

1. Fred P. Graham, "Supreme Court Agrees to Rule on Printing of Vietnam Series: Arguments to be Heard Today" (*The New York Times,* June 26, 1971), p. 1-10.

2. *The New York Times* (June 27, 1971), p. 24.

3. Ibid.

4. Ibid.

5. Ibid., p. 25.

6. Ibid.

7. Ibid.

8. Ibid.

9. Ibid., pp. 25-26.

10. Ibid., p. 26.

11. Ibid.

12. Ibid.

13. Ibid.

Chapter 6

1. Graham, "Supreme Court Weighs Issues on Vietnam Series After Pleas: Rejects a U.S. Secrecy Request" (*The New York Times,* June 27, 1971)p. 1-1.

2. *United States of America* v. *New York Times Company,* et al. (Per Curiam Opinion, U.S. Supreme Court, June 30, 1971), p. 1.

3. *United States of America* v. *New York Times Company*, et al. (Dissenting Opinions, Justice Burger, Blackmun, and Harlan, U.S. Supreme Court, June 30, 1971).

4. *United States of America* v. *New York Times Company*, et al. (Majority Opinions, June 30, 1971).

5. *United States of America* v. *New York Times Company*, et al. (Opinion of Justice Black, June 30, 1971), p. 4.

6. *United States of America* v. *New York Times Company*, et al. (Opinion of Justice Douglas, June 30, 1971), pp. 4-5.

7. *United States of America* v. *New York Times Company*, et al. (Opinion of Justice Stewart, June 30, 1971), p. 4.

8. *United States of America* v. *New York Times Company*, et al. (Opinion of Justice Marshall, June 30, 1971), p. 3.

9. Graham, "Supreme Court, 6-3, Upholds Newspapers: Times Resumes its Series Halted 15 Days on Publication of the Pentagon Report" (*The New York Times*, July 1, 1971), p. 1-15.

10. Ibid.

11. Graham, "Supreme Court Weighs Issues on Vietnam Series After Pleas: Rejects a U.S. Secrecy Request" (*The New York Times*, June 27, 1971) pp. 1-15.

Further Reading

Berger, Raoul. *Congress* v. *The Supreme Court.* New York: Bantam Books, 1973.

Bickel, Alexander M. *The Morality of Consent.* New Haven, CT: Yale University Press, 1975.

Friendly, Fred W., and Martha J. H. Elliott, *The Constitution: That Delicate Balance.* New York: Random House, 1984.

New York Times Company v. *United States.* New York: Arno Press, 1971.

Tribe, Laurence H. *God Save This Honorable Court: How the Choice of Justices Can Change Our Lives.* New York: Random House, 1985.

Weiss, Ann, *The Supreme Court.* Hillside, NJ: Enslow, 1987.

Woodward, Bob, and Scott Armstrong. *The Brethren: Inside the Supreme Court.* New York: Simon & Schuster, 1979.

Index

V

W

Y